Contents

The girl with nothing to do   4

Florence makes a decision   8

A useful meeting   10

Devotion to duty   14

The Lady with the Lamp   16

The work goes on   22

The Nightingale Nurses   25

Glossary   30

Date chart   31

Books to read   31

Index   32

Words printed in **bold** appear in the glossary.

The girl with nothing to do

Above Lea Hurst, the Nightingales' family home in Derbyshire.

The city of Florence in Italy always had special meaning for Fanny Nightingale and her husband William. It was there, on 12 May 1820, that their second child was born. They decided to name her Florence, after the beautiful city where she was born. In those days it was unusual to name a baby after a city. But Florence grew up to become an unusual woman.

The beautiful city of Florence, Italy.

Life Stories
Florence Nightingale

Nina Morgan

Illustrated by Gavin Rowe

HODDER
Wayland

an imprint of Hodder Chi

Life Stories

Gandi
Florence Nightingale

For more information on this series and other Hodder Wayland titles,
go to www.hodderwayland.co.uk

Cover and frontispiece: *A photograph
of Florence Nightingale as a young woman.*

Editor: Anna Girling
Consultant: Nigel Smith
Designer: Loraine Hayes

First published in Great Britain in 1992 by
Wayland Publishers Ltd
Reprinted in 2001, 2002, 2003 and 2004 by Hodder Wayland,
an imprint of Hodder Children's Books

British Library Cataloguing in Publication Data
Morgan, Nina
Florence Nightingale.—(Life Stories Series)
I. Title   II. Rowe, Gavin   III. Series
610.73092

PAPERBACK ISBN 0-7502-1678-6

Typeset by Dorchester Typesetting Group Ltd
Printed in China by WKT Company Limited.

Hodder Children's Books
A division of Hodder Headline Limited
338 Euston Road
London NW1 3BH

Florence Nightingale was born into a rich English family, but she was a very unhappy girl. When she was young, most girls like Florence spent their time visiting friends and going to parties. Their parents hoped they would meet a rich husband who could look after them. Fanny Nightingale wanted this sort of life for Florence and her older sister Parthenope.

Florence as a young woman, with her sister Parthenope (standing).

But Florence had other ideas. She knew there was more to life than parties and dances.

When she was sixteen years old Florence believed she heard the voice of God. She thought God was calling her to do special work. She did not know what the job was, but she knew that she must try to find a way to be useful. Florence did not dare tell anyone about God's message.

The sons and daughters of rich people spent their time visiting friends.

Soon afterwards, the Nightingales left for a tour of Europe that lasted nearly two years. Florence enjoyed her trip, but she still believed that God had other ideas for her.

7

Florence makes a decision

Florence waited nearly two years before she thought she knew what God wanted her to do. She decided she must help poor, hungry and sick people. But how could she do this?

Florence began by taking food, **medicines** and clothes to sick people near where she lived. But when she asked if she could go to learn how to nurse at a hospital in Salisbury, near her home in

A hospital in 1808. In those days hospitals often lacked equipment.

southern England, her parents were shocked and angry.

It is easy to see why. Hospitals in those days were crowded, dirty and smelly. Nurses were usually uneducated women. They were often drunk, and knew little about caring for the sick.

In spite of her parent's feelings Florence was determined. For the next two years, she got up early to study medicine in secret. Then, when she was twenty-seven, her family sent her to Europe to try to make her forget her silly ideas.

A useful meeting

Sidney Herbert.

Florence went to stay with some friends in Rome in Italy. There she met Sidney Herbert, a rich Englishman who believed that people with money should help the poor and sick.

He introduced Florence to others who felt the same way. Instead of making her forget about nursing, her time in Rome made Florence return to England more determined than ever to work in a hospital.

Some years earlier, when Florence was twenty-two, a successful **journalist** called Richard Monckton Milnes had asked Florence to marry him. She made him wait seven years for her reply. Although she loved him, Florence now refused his **proposal**. She believed her work was more important than marriage.

A portrait of Florence, drawn by her sister.

Florence's parents were very angry and upset. In the mid-1800s, no well-brought up girl would dream of earning her own money by working outside her home. A woman like Florence would never choose to work in a hospital, alongside rude nurses and surrounded by filthy, suffering, sick people.

Kaiserswerth Institution.

To try to make their daughter see sense, the Nightingales once again sent Florence to Europe. In Germany she discovered the Kaiserswerth Institution. Here, religious single women and **widows**, all from good families, worked as nurses or teachers to help the sick and mentally ill.

In 1851, when she was thirty-one years old, Florence persuaded her parents to let her work at the Kaiserswerth Institution for three months. Although the hours were long and hard, Florence wrote home, saying: 'I am as happy as the day is long.'

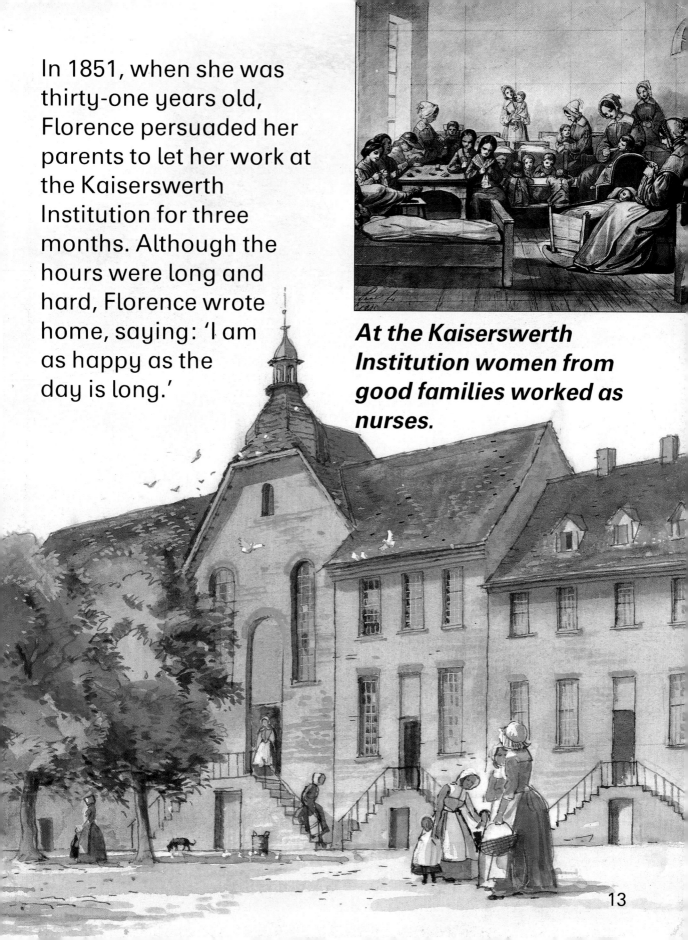

At the Kaiserswerth Institution women from good families worked as nurses.

Devotion to duty

When Florence arrived back home she discovered her father, sister and grandmother were ill. Instead of working in a hospital, Florence spent the next two years nursing them.

Although she was very busy, she continued working at her studies and visited hospitals in London, Edinburgh, Dublin and Paris.

Below *In crowded, dirty cities diseases like cholera spread rapidly.*

When she was thirty-three, Florence took a job running a private hospital for 'sick **gentlewomen**' in London. Her mother was horrified, but her father stood up for her. He gave her some money – £500 per year – to live on.

The next year, Florence offered to nurse people suffering from **cholera**. The work was dangerous and hard, but Florence was happy.

The Lady with the Lamp

In 1854 the **Crimean War** broke out. The Crimea is a piece of land that sticks out into the Black Sea. The Turks and the Russians were at war. The British and the French sent soldiers to the Crimea to help the

Bloody battles were fought in the Crimea.

Turks. The battles were fierce and bloody.

A newspaper journalist for *The Times* sent back horrifying stories from the war. Thousands of British soldiers were dying because there was not enough medical help. He called for nurses to travel to the Crimea.

This picture shows French soldiers in the Crimea.

One of the nurses who worked in Scutari.

Florence's old friend Sidney Herbert was now a member of the government and in charge of the war effort. She wrote to him to offer her help. Herbert asked Florence to collect a party of nurses to go to the Crimea. This was the first time a woman had been asked to do such an important job.

It was very difficult to find good, trained nurses but finally Florence made up a group of thirty-eight women. She ordered supplies and was given some money sent by readers of *The Times*.

When the nurses arrived at the hospital at Scutari, in Turkey, they were shocked by what they found. The hospital was filthy and the drains were blocked. The wounded lay on the floors, dressed in bloody rags. Rats and fleas were everywhere. There was little food.

Worst of all, the army doctors were not pleased to see them. They would not let them visit the sick. Florence put her nurses to work checking stores and sewing – and waited.

The journey to the Crimea was long and hard. The nurses suffered from seasickness.

19

The nurses improved conditions by cleaning the filthy hospital.

She did not have to wait long. Soon the wounded began pouring into the hospital. The army doctors were **overwhelmed** and, at last, they asked Florence and her nurses to help.

Florence set her nurses to work cleaning the hospital. She took on

local people to unblock the drains, and used the money from *The Times* to buy food and supplies. In just a few weeks Florence had greatly improved conditions at the hospital.

Florence often worked for twenty hours a day. The men called her the 'Lady with the Lamp' because every night she walked through the **wards** to comfort the sick.

By the time the war ended in 1856, Florence was a national heroine in Britain. But she was not interested in fame. She

Every night in the wards, Florence carried a Turkish lamp like this one.

travelled home in secret. When she arrived, only the family housekeeper was there to meet her.

The work goes on

Back in Britain, Florence received sackfuls of letters, but only one was important to her. This was a letter from Queen Victoria, inviting Florence to visit her at her castle at Balmoral, in Scotland.

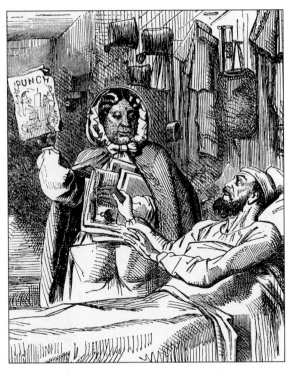

Mary Seacole, a Jamaican, also nursed soldiers in the Crimea. She too met Queen Victoria after the war.

Queen Victoria, who agreed to help Florence improve army hospitals.

When Florence met the Queen, Florence talked about her ideas for improving army hospitals in England. Queen Victoria agreed to give her help.

As a result of Florence's work, an army medical college was set up in Chatham in Kent and a military hospital was set up in London.

Florence was also interested in health problems in India, which was part of the **British Empire**. She wanted to improve the health of British soldiers there. She was also worried about the health of poor people in India. As a result of Florence's work, a health department was set up.

News of Florence's work became known throughout the world.

Thousands of soldiers were wounded in the American Civil War.

During the **Civil War** in the USA, Florence was asked for advice about caring for the wounded. She sent many reports and instructions.

When the war was over, an important American wrote to Florence: 'Your influence and our debt to you can never be known.'

The Nightingale Nurses

Florence refused to accept any honours when she returned from the Crimea. But she did accept a job setting up the world's first training school for nurses.

The Nightingale School for Nurses was set up at St Thomas's Hospital in London in 1860. Nurses are still trained there today. Florence did not teach at the school, but instead provided much advice. The rules she made were very strict. To help in the organization of the new training school, Florence wrote a book called *Notes on Nursing*.

Florence surrounded by student nurses at the Nightingale School.

For many years, Florence worked from her bed.

Many Nightingale Nurses went on to work abroad and introduced Florence's ideas in other countries. Her methods form an important part of nursing training today.

By the time Florence was forty-three, she was so worn out that she had to spend much of her time in bed. But she carried on writing letters and reports, and important people came to her bedside to talk about health improvements.

The new St Thomas's Hospital, opened in 1871.

In 1907, King Edward VII awarded Florence the **Order of Merit**. This was the first time this great honour had ever been given to a woman.

Florence Nightingale died in 1910, when she was ninety years old. The British people wanted to honour her with a great funeral and burial in Westminster Abbey in London. But in her **will** Florence asked for something different.

Florence's funeral took place in the Hampshire village near where she lived.

Florence got her last wish, and lies buried in a simple grave in a churchyard in Hampshire, near one of her family's homes.

Florence never wanted to be famous, but her work in training nurses and improving conditions in hospitals means that she will never be forgotten.

Florence's tombstone gives only her initials and the dates of her birth and death.

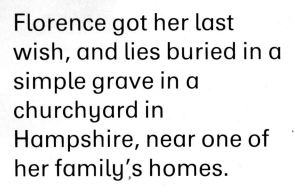

Glossary

British Empire All the countries controlled by Britain. The British Empire no longer exists, but in the 19th century it included many countries.

Cholera A serious illness which causes diarrhoea and cramps.

Civil War A civil war is a war between two sets of people from the same country. The American Civil War lasted from 1861 to 1865.

Crimean War A war fought between 1854 and 1856, in which the British and the French helped the Turks fight against the Russians.

Gentlewomen Women from rich family backgrounds.

Journalist A person who writes for newspapers.

Medicines Substances that sick people swallow or rub on their skin to cure them. Medicine also means the study of illnesses.

Order of Merit An award given by the British king or queen to honour people for their services to the country.

Overwhelmed Unable to cope.

Proposal Asking someone to marry.

Wards The rooms full of beds in a hospital.

Widow A woman whose husband has died.

Will A document in which people say what they want to happen to their possessions after they die.

Date chart

1820 Florence Nightingale born on 12 May.

1837 Florence believes she hears a call from God.

1847 Meets Sidney Herbert in Rome.

1849 Refuses proposal of marriage.

1851 Works in the Kaiserswerth Institution in Germany.

1853 Runs a hospital for 'sick gentlewomen' in London.

1854 Takes a group of nurses to the Crimea.

1856 Returns to England.

1860 The Nightingale School for Nurses set up at St Thomas's Hospital in London.

1861–65 Advises on caring for the wounded in the American Civil War.

1907 Awarded the Order of Merit.

1910 Florence dies on 13 August.

Books to read

Florence Nightingale by Angela Bull (Hamish Hamilton, 1985)
Florence Nightingale by Richard Tames (Franklin Watts, 2003)

For older readers:
Groundbreakers: Florence Nightingale by John Malam (Heinemann, 2001)

Index

American Civil War 24

Crimean War 16-21

Herbert, Sidney 10, 18
hospitals 8-9, 11, 15, 18, 20-2, 24-6
    army hospitals 22, 24
    hospital for sick gentlewomen 15
    St Thomas's Hospital 25-6
    Scutari Hospital 18, 20-21

Kaiserswerth Institution 12-13

Nightingale, Florence
    birth 4
    parents 4-5, 9, 11
    message from God 7
    tours of Europe 7, 9, 12
    studies 9, 14
    marriage proposal 10-11
    work in the Crimea 18-21
    setting up of training school 25
    ill-health 26
    awarded Order of Merit 28
    death 28
    funeral 28-9
Nightingale Nurses, the 25-6
Notes on Nursing 25

Scutari 18, 20-21
Seacole, Mary 22

Victoria, Queen 22

Picture acknowledgements
The publishers would like to thank the following: Billie Love Collection 12; Florence Nightingale Museum 16, 17, 20, 21, 25, 26 (top); Hampshire Record Office 28; Hulton-Deutsch Collection 11, 26 (bottom); Mansell Collection 10; Mary Evans Picture Library 7, 14, 22 (top and bottom); Peter Newark's Historical Pictures cover and frontispiece, 5, 18; PHOTRI 24; Wellcome Institute Library, London 8; Zefa 4.